Hymns of Heaven
A Hospice Devotional

Sarah Esquivel

Contents

Introduction

I want to start by introducing myself. My name is Sarah and I have the privilege of serving as a hospice chaplain. Serving in this role has invited me into one of the most holy places on earth, and that is the portal between heaven and earth. As I sit with a person transitioning from this life to the next, it is as if the fragrance of heaven literally invades the earth (and I believe it does!).

I have seen people come from a place of total unbelief to full faith and trust in Jesus. I have seen people go from fear and uncertainty to peace and assurance. I have even been able to pray with people as they breathe their last breath. There is nothing like sitting with someone as they walk across the finish line. It is truly a privilege to be invited into that space with a person and their loved ones.

One thing I have discovered is that it can be challenging for people to pinpoint what causes anxiety or uneasiness about death. It can also be hard for loved ones to approach such a deep subject. By writing this devotional, it is my hope that it provides a resource to help people navigate the places in their hearts (and/or hearts of their loved ones) that can be hard to talk through when it comes time to transition from this life to eternity.

Even if you or a loved one still have years left on this earth, this devotional will be a great way to dive in and find peace in your heart when thinking about the things of eternity. It will help you live with a new sense of peace and purpose.

You will notice that each week has a hymn associated with it. I have found that singing hymns together is a very significant way that people connect to the Lord and find peace in His presence even through sickness and disease. I recorded each hymn that goes along with this devotional and I encourage you to take time each day to listen to the hymn associated with that devotional and sing along. **You can find each hymn on this YouTube playlist along with the words to sing along. To listen to the songs, you can scan the QR code below or use this link:** https://tinyurl.com/39ss6bnd

There is a prayer for every devotional as well as a final prayer to pray over someone who is about to transition into the next life at the very end of the book.

I wish I could be there face-to-face with each one of you to pray with you and offer a hug of encouragement as you walk through this journey. I pray that this devotional is a source of hope and offers meaningful conversations for each one of you.

God bless you!

- Sarah

Week 1: Jesus Made a Way

SONG FOR THE WEEK - The Old Rugged Cross (1912)

VERSE 1:
On a hill far away stood an old rugged cross
The emblem of suffering and shame
And I love that old cross where the dearest and best
For a world of lost sinners was slain
CHORUS:
So I'll cherish the old rugged cross
Till my trophies at last I lay down
I will cling to the old rugged cross
And exchange it someday for a crown
VERSE 2:
In the old rugged cross, stained with blood so divine
A wondrous beauty I see
For 'twas on that old cross Jesus suffered and died
To pardon and sanctify me
VERSE 3:
To the old rugged cross I will ever be true
It's shame and reproach gladly bear
Then he'll call me some day to my home far away
Where his glory forever I'll share

Day 1 - What the Cross Did for Us

"In the old rugged cross, stained with blood so divine
A wondrous beauty I see
For 'twas on that old cross Jesus suffered and died
To pardon and sanctify me"

John 3:16 - For God so loved the world that he gave his one and only Son, that whoever believes in him shall not perish but have eternal life.

Acts 4:12 - Salvation is found in no one else, for there is no other name under heaven given to mankind by which we must be saved.

Isaiah 53:4-6 - Surely he took up our pain and bore our suffering, yet we considered him punished by God, stricken by him, and afflicted. But he was pierced for our transgressions, he was crushed for our iniquities; the punishment that brought us peace was on him, and by his wounds we are healed. We all, like sheep, have gone astray, each of us has turned to our own way; and the Lord has laid on him the iniquity of us all.

Our heavenly Father is always motivated by love. It was love that caused Him to send his one and only Son into the world in order to save us. Jesus made a way for us to know the Father, and to spend eternity with Him by what He did for us on the cross.

On the cross, Jesus bore our sin and offered Himself as the perfect sacrifice to God. Because of the blood that Jesus shed, we now can approach God directly. Jesus was pierced for our sins. The punishment that He endured is what brings us peace today, and because of the wounds of Jesus we are healed.

The cross changed everything. It made a way for us to approach God directly. It provided forgiveness for our sins and healing for us in every way—physically, spiritually and emotionally.

Father God - We thank you for sending your only Son to take our place. We recognize that He is the only true way to you. We pray that you would show us how to walk fully in all that He purchased for us on the cross.

In the name of Jesus, Amen.

Questions:

1. **When you think about heaven, do you think that you need to do something to earn your way in?**

2. **Salvation is a free gift offered to us by Jesus. It is available to everyone, but we have to be willing to receive it. Have you received that free gift of salvation through Jesus?**

   a. **If Yes - When do you remember salvation becoming personal and real for you?**

   a. **If No or Unsure - I invite you to take some time to thank God for Jesus and receive the salvation and forgiveness that only comes through Him.**

Day 2 - All are Welcome

Isaiah 61:1 The Spirit of the Sovereign Lord is on me, because the Lord has anointed me to proclaim good news to the poor. He has sent me to bind up the brokenhearted, to proclaim freedom for the captives and release from darkness for the prisoners.

Luke 23:39-43 One of the criminals who hung there hurled insults at him: "Aren't you the Messiah? Save yourself and us!" But the other criminal rebuked him. "Don't you fear God," he said, "since you are under the same sentence? We are punished justly, for we are getting what our deeds deserve. But this man has done nothing wrong." Then he said, "Jesus, remember me when you come into your kingdom." Jesus answered him, "Truly I tell you, today you will be with me in paradise."

Everyone is welcome to receive the gift of salvation that is available through Jesus. It doesn't matter what anyone's life has looked like. Jesus was sent to bind up the brokenhearted, to proclaim freedom to the captives and release prisoners from darkness.

I don't know if you are someone who has gone to church your entire life or someone who resonates more with the criminal hanging on the cross next to Jesus but it doesn't matter; the same gift of salvation is available for all of us.

If you are someone who has attended church for a long time, join me as we encourage those new to the faith and welcome them into the family! Look for opportunities to show new believers the love of God.

If you are new to church or have a long history of sin in your life, I encourage you to move forward in the forgiveness and healing through Jesus today rather than fixating on the past.

There is forgiveness and salvation available for all! Make sure that you aren't counting yourself or others out because of what you see. Jesus told the criminal next to Him that He would be with Jesus in paradise, and we need to have that same understanding. In a moment God can change anyone.

Father God - Thank you that you made a way for all people to know you. Help me to love all people and show them your love. Help me to let go of the sin in my past and focus on moving forward and being a light to those around me.

In the name of Jesus, Amen.

Questions:

1. **Do you resonate more with the person who has attended church your whole life or the criminal on the cross?**

   a. **Church Goer - Is it hard for you to love those that are different from you, especially when they have major sin in their life?**

   b. **Non Church Goer/New to Church - Do you find it hard to let go of your past and receive the forgiveness that God provides which is free of shame and guilt?**

Day 3 - Being Hated for the Cross

"To the old rugged cross I will ever be true
It's shame and reproach gladly bear
Then he'll call me some day to my home far away
Where his glory forever I'll share"

John 15:18-19 - If the world hates you, keep in mind that it hated me first. If you belonged to the world, it would love you as its own. As it is, you do not belong to the world, but I have chosen you out of the world. That is why the world hates you.

Romans 1:16a - For I am not ashamed of the gospel, because it is the power of God that brings salvation to everyone who believes.

It is important to realize that we do not belong to this world and that it is not our permanent home. With that in mind, we should not live lives that are meant to get the most out of this world but should instead be investing in the life to come. The world hated Jesus. We should not be surprised when we are rejected by people for what we believe or even hated because what we believe is offensive.

We must live lives that are unashamed of the Gospel because it truly is the only thing that has the power to save everyone who believes. If we are ashamed of Jesus in front of people, a few things happen: 1) Jesus will be ashamed of us in front of the Father (Luke 9:26) and 2) We don't let God use us to invite others into the only thing that has the power to save their souls.

I wish that we could live lives where we always get along with everyone, but the reality is that the gospel is offensive. We should love at all times but also be ready to be rejected and even hated for the gospel of Jesus Christ.

Father God - Help me to focus on the things of eternity rather than getting consumed by the things of earth. Show me who is in front of me that you are asking me to share the gospel with. Give me the words to say and the love that only you give.

In the name of Jesus, Amen.

Questions:

1. **Have you ever been rejected by someone because of your faith in Jesus?**

2. **What stops you from sharing your faith with others?**

3. **What have you found to be the easiest way for you to share your faith?**

Day 4 - It is Finished

*"So I'll cherish the old rugged cross
Till my trophies at last I lay down
I will cling to the old rugged cross
And exchange it someday for a crown"*

John 19:30 - When he had received the drink, Jesus said, "It is finished." With that, he bowed his head and gave up his spirit.

Titus 3:4-7 - But when the kindness and love of God our Savior appeared, he saved us, not because of righteous things we had done, but because of his mercy. He saved us through the washing of rebirth and renewal by the Holy Spirit, whom he poured out on us generously through Jesus Christ our Savior, so that, having been justified by his grace, we might become heirs having the hope of eternal life.

Jesus accomplished all that needed to be done for us. We are saved not because of the righteous things that we have done, but because of the mercy of God. There is nothing that we can do to earn our way into heaven.

This is good news! We do not have the capability to be *good enough* to earn our way to God which is why He sent His son to take our place. This doesn't mean that what we believe shouldn't be reflected in our lives. James clearly says "faith by itself, if it is not accompanied by action, is dead" (James 2:17).

If we aren't motivated to love and serve those around us, then our faith is dead and we need to ask God to bring it back to life. Ask God to show you what opportunities He is putting in front of you to exercise your faith. The world becomes much more exciting when we live this way!

Father God - We thank you that you did everything that needed to be done in order for us to be saved. Forgive us for thinking that we somehow earn it ourselves. Forgive us when we try to earn your love by performing for you. Help us to be motivated to good works by love for people. Show us the opportunities that you are putting in front of us to show others your love and truth.

In the name of Jesus, Amen.

Questions:

1. **Who is a person that you remember in your life who had a passion for God and a love for people? How did that person impact you?**

2. **The song says, "So I'll cherish the old rugged cross, till my trophies at last I lay down." What are some of the things that you are most proud of in this life?**

Day 5 - We can be Certain of Heaven

"On a hill far away stood an old rugged cross
The emblem of suffering and shame
And I love that old cross where the dearest and best
For a world of lost sinners was slain"

John 5:24 - Very truly I tell you, whoever hears my word and believes him who sent me has eternal life and will not be judged but has crossed over from death to life.

Romans 10:9-10 - If you declare with your mouth, "Jesus is Lord," and believe in your heart that God raised him from the dead, you will be saved. For it is with your heart that you believe and are justified, and it is with your mouth that you profess your faith and are saved.

As a hospice chaplain, I have talked to so many people who are facing death and they are not quite sure if they are going to heaven. These are people who know Jesus and have accepted Him as their Lord and Savior, yet they still don't know for sure where they are headed. There is often an underlying belief that they didn't do enough or weren't good enough to get in.

We have talked about how we cannot earn our way into heaven, and today I want to reflect on scriptures that tell us plainly that we are saved simply through our faith in Jesus.

My desire is that no one reading this would get done with today's reading and still have doubt in their heart about heaven. We are told very clearly that it is by declaring that Jesus is Lord and by believing in our heart that God raised Him from the dead that we are saved. God did not intend to make this process complicated for us. He wants us to know Him and to spend eternity with Him.

I encourage you to go to God with your doubt and ask Him to replace it with faith. There is no need to fear what comes next. We can look forward to it with eager anticipation knowing that we will get to be with God face-to-face!

Father God - Thank you for the gift of salvation. Help us to receive this free gift. We acknowledge that doubt comes into our minds at times. We ask that you would help us combat this doubt and replace it with the truth of your word. Give us assurance that we will be with you in heaven.

In the name of Jesus, Amen.

Questions:

1. **Do you believe that Jesus is the way to the Father?**

2. **Do you believe that God raised Him from the dead?**

3. **When you think about eternity do you feel peace, anxiousness or something in the middle?**

Week 2: The Faithfulness of God

SONG FOR THE WEEK - Great is Thy Faithfulness

VERSE 1:
Great is Thy faithfulness, O God my Father
There is no shadow of turning with Thee
Thou changest not, Thy compassions, they fail not
As Thou hast been Thou forever wilt be
CHORUS:
Great is Thy faithfulness, great is Thy faithfulness
Morning by morning new mercies I see
All I have needed Thy hand hath provided
Great is Thy faithfulness, Lord, unto me
VERSE 2:
Summer and winter, and springtime and harvest
Sun, moon and stars in their courses above
Join with all nature in manifold witness
To Thy great faithfulness, mercy and love
VERSE 3:
Pardon for sin and a peace that endureth
Thine own dear presence to cheer and to guide
Strength for today and bright hope for tomorrow
Blessings all mine, with ten thousand beside

Day 1 - God is not Like People

"Great is Thy faithfulness, O God my Father
There is no shadow of turning with Thee
Thou changest not, Thy compassions, they fail not
As Thou hast been Thou forever wilt be"

Numbers 23:19 - God is not man, that he should lie, or a son of man, that he should change his mind. Has he said, and will he not do it? Or has he spoken, and will he not fulfill it?

2 Timothy 2:13 - If we are faithless, he remains faithful, for he cannot disown himself.

It's easy to see God the same way that we see people. People have let us down so we assume God will too. People have not kept their word to us so we assume God will do the same. People have abandoned us so we assume God will as well.

We must remember that God is not like people. He is faithful. He shows up when no else does. He keeps His word. If He said it, He will do it. Our God never changes. He is the same yesterday, today and forever (Hebrews 13:8).

Some of us may feel like we have not been faithful to God in our lives and that because of that, He will give up on us. The truth is that even when we are unfaithful, God remains faithful.

Father God - We thank you for your faithfulness. We know that you are not like people. You do not say one thing and do another. We also thank you that in spite of our shortcomings you continue to remain faithful in our lives. We thank you for all of the ways that you have been faithful to us. Open our eyes to see your faithfulness today.

In the name of Jesus, Amen.

Questions:

1. **What are the main characteristics of God in your eyes?**

2. **How has God been faithful to you even when people were not faithful in your life?**

Day 2 - God has not Forgotten You

Jeremiah 29:11-13 - "For I know the plans I have for you," declares the Lord, "plans to prosper you and not to harm you, plans to give you hope and a future. Then you will call on me and come and pray to me, and I will listen to you. You will seek me and find me when you seek me with all your heart."

Philippians 1:6 - And I am sure of this, that he who began a good work in you will bring it to completion at the day of Jesus Christ.

Your purpose is not finished. If you still have breath in your lungs, there is still something God intends to do *in* you and *through* you. This understanding adds new intentionality to your day.

There are opportunities that God has placed in front of you to be His hands and His feet to those around you. These people could be family members, coworkers, caregivers, grocery store workers…the list goes on. Don't overcomplicate it. Being the hands and feet of Jesus could be as simple as a smile or a kind word to someone.

Remember, God is faithful. He has not forgotten you or given up on you. As you surrender yourself to Him afresh, He will reveal what He has for you today.

Father God - We thank you for your faithfulness in our lives. You have not forgotten us. You still have a purpose and a plan for us. We want to be obedient to what you are asking of us. We know we don't exist simply to serve ourselves. Help us to see the opportunities that you place in front of us today. We give ourselves to you.

In the name of Jesus, Amen.

Questions:

1. **Do you feel like God still has a purpose for you?**

2. **What opportunities has God given you lately to show people His love?**

Day 3 - When Everything Else Fails, God Does Not

"Pardon for sin and a peace that endureth
Thine own dear presence to cheer and to guide
Strength for today and bright hope for tomorrow
Blessings all mine, with ten thousand beside"

John 16:33 - I have told you these things, so that in me you may have peace. In this world you will have trouble. But take heart! I have overcome the world.

2 Corinthians 12:9 - But he said to me, "My grace is sufficient for you, for my power is made perfect in weakness." Therefore I will boast all the more gladly about my weaknesses, so that Christ's power may rest on me.

Some days it feels like everything around us is failing. Our bodies might fail us. Relationships might fall apart. Something comes out of nowhere that we were not expecting. In moments like this, we have a choice. We can try and take control of the situation or we can turn control over to God.

There is comfort in knowing that while we face all kinds of trouble, Jesus has overcome it all. God is bigger than anything that we are up against and He will never fail us.

When you feel weak, talk to God about it. Ask Him to give you *His* strength. His power truly works best in our weakness.

Father God - We thank you that you are faithful even when everything around us seems to fall apart. We recognize that you have overcome the world. Our hope rests in you and you alone. We admit that we feel weak and we ask for your strength to rest on us today.

In the name of Jesus, Amen.

Questions:

1. **Are there situations in your life right now that bring you trouble?**

2. **Have you been able to surrender those situations to God or do you feel like you're still holding on to them? What can you do to let go?**

Day 4 - Creation Testifies to God's Faithfulness

"Summer and winter, and springtime and harvest
Sun, moon and stars in their courses above
Join with all nature in manifold witness
To Thy great faithfulness, mercy and love"

Psalm 19:1-4a - The heavens declare the glory of God; the skies proclaim the work of his hands. Day after day they pour forth speech; night after night they reveal knowledge. They have no speech, they use no words; no sound is heard from them. Yet their voice goes out into all the earth, their words to the ends of the world.

Psalm 86:15 - But you, Lord, are a compassionate and gracious God, slow to anger, abounding in love and faithfulness.

Think for a moment about how the sun comes up every morning and goes down every night. Reflect on the seasons throughout the year. Each year we have spring, summer, winter and fall. God designed creation in such a way that it gives witness to His faithfulness.

Just as you can count on the sun rising and setting each day, you can count on God to show up in your life. He will provide for you in every way. He will comfort you and counsel you. He will watch over you and protect you.

Take time today to notice God's creation. Allow it to be a witness in your heart to the faithfulness of God. Our God is compassionate and gracious, slow to anger and abounding in love and faithfulness.

Father God - We thank you for your faithfulness. We know that no matter what needs we have that you will meet them. It may not be how we anticipated, but your ways are good and we trust you. Help us to slow down enough to see your hand in creation and to allow it to remind us of your faithfulness.

In the name of Jesus, Amen.

Questions:

1. **What are some of your favorite parts of God's creation? (Sunsets/sunrises, stars, animals, flowers, etc.)**

2. **God's creation is truly beautiful and the world that He created is nothing short of amazing. Where is your favorite place that you have traveled to?**

Day 5 - It's a New Day!

"Great is Thy faithfulness, great is Thy faithfulness
Morning by morning new mercies I see
All I have needed Thy hand hath provided
Great is Thy faithfulness, Lord, unto me"

Lamentations 2:22-23 - Because of the Lord's great love we are not consumed, for his compassions never fail. They are new every morning; great is your faithfulness.

Hebrews 4:16 - Let us then approach God's throne of grace with confidence, so that we may receive mercy and find grace to help us in our time of need.

There is so much joy when we realize that God has new mercy for us every day. No matter what yesterday looked like or this past year has looked like, God has new strength and mercy for us today.

Because of Jesus, we can approach God with confidence and receive the mercy that we need to help us in our time of need. It is important that we actually approach Him. So often we go through struggles in life and we never go to God for the strength that we need.

Jesus made a way for us to go directly to God in prayer. You may be wondering where God is in your life, but He may be waiting for you to come to Him. Let's realign our focus and our hearts today as we approach God's throne of grace.

Father God - We thank you for new mercy each day. We know that you see us and see the needs that we have, but you desire that we come to you with those needs. We ask for mercy and grace for today. We won't get consumed with tomorrow, but instead we will focus on today. Thank you that you are with us and are giving us the strength we need.

In the name of Jesus, Amen.

Questions:

1. **What do you think your future has in store for you?**

   a. **Are there things about the future that make you feel unsettled? If so, what are those things?**

2. **What are some things that happened in the past year or even week that have been challenging (areas where you need new mercies)?**

3. **Who have you known that has modeled prayer well?**

Week 3: What a Friend

SONG FOR THE WEEK - What a Friend We Have in Jesus

VERSE 1:
What a friend we have in Jesus
All our sins and griefs to bear
What a privilege to carry
Everything to God in prayer
O what peace we often forfeit
O what needless pain we bear
All because we do not carry
Everything to God in prayer
VERSE 2:
Have we trials and temptations
Is there trouble anywhere
We should never be discouraged
Take it to the Lord in prayer
Can we find a friend so faithful
Who will all our sorrows share
Jesus knows our every weakness
Take it to the Lord in prayer
VERSE 3:
Are we weak and heavy-laden
Cumbered with a load of care
Precious Savior, still our refuge
Take it to the Lord in prayer
Do thy friends despise, forsake thee
Take it to the Lord in prayer
In His arms He'll take and shield thee
Thou wilt find a solace there

Day 1 - Prayer Equals Peace

"O what peace we often forfeit
O what needless pain we bear
All because we do not carry
Everything to God in prayer"

Philippians 4:6-7 - Do not be anxious about anything, but in every situation, by prayer and petition, with thanksgiving, present your requests to God. And the peace of God, which transcends all understanding, will guard your hearts and your minds in Christ Jesus.

Isaiah 26:3 - You will keep in perfect peace all who trust in you, all whose thoughts are fixed on you!

When I sing the song *What a Friend We Have in Jesus* the main thing I am reminded of is to turn to God in prayer in every situation. When life is great, sometimes we neglect to pray because things seem to be going so well. When storms hit in life, sometimes we neglect to pray because we are simply overwhelmed. When life is going normal, sometimes we neglect to pray because we are bored with the mundaneness of our days.

We must be intentional in our prayer life. When we are intentional about prayer, we experience a supernatural peace that only God can provide. When we put into practice what this song says, which is that Jesus is our friend, it makes it easier for us to talk to Him each day.

No matter what is going on in your life, God wants you to bring Him into it. If prayer isn't a normal part of your day, I encourage you to change that starting today. Prayer is simply talking to God; remember He is your friend.

Father God - We thank you that we can come to you with anything that is happening in our lives. We thank you for the peace that only you can give. We pray that you would replace worry and fear with your peace today. We give you the situations that weigh us down and we trust you with them.

In the name of Jesus, Amen.

Questions:

1. **Is prayer a regular part of your life?**

2. **Are you comfortable going to God in prayer or is it a bit awkward for you?**

3. **Are there things today that you would like to surrender to Him in order to experience His peace? If so, what are they?**

Day 2 - Jesus Calls Us Friend

"What a Friend we have in Jesus
All our sins and griefs to bear
What a privilege to carry
Everything to God in prayer"

Romans 5:11 - So now we can rejoice in our wonderful new relationship with God because our Lord Jesus Christ has made us friends of God.

John 15:13-15 - Greater love has no one than this: to lay down one's life for one's friends. You are my friends if you do what I command. I no longer call you servants, because a servant does not know his master's business. Instead, I have called you friends, for everything that I learned from my Father I have made known to you.

Exodus 33:11 - The Lord would speak to Moses face to face, as one speaks to a friend.

It is truly remarkable to think of ourselves as friends of God. It adds a new level of intimacy and closeness to our relationship with Him. A good friend is someone who you can be your truest self around. It is someone who stands by you through life's ups and downs. A good friend is someone who always has your best interests at heart. God is this type of friend.

Our faith must go beyond some sort of religious obligation and enter into a real relationship with God. He desires that we talk to Him, read

His word and live in a way that pleases Him. As we do that, our relationship with Him grows deeper and we learn His voice more clearly.

What a privilege it is to be called a friend of God! Let us not take that for granted, but instead let's work to grow our relationship with Him each day.

Father God - We thank you that you are not a God who is far off in the distance, but instead that you are a God who is near to us. You desire closeness with us and we want that with you as well. Thank you for loving us like only you can. There is no friend like you.

In the name of Jesus, Amen.

Questions:

1. **Have you seen yourself as God's friend or is this a new concept for you?**

2. **How does seeing yourself as a friend of God change the way you see your relationship with Him?**

Day 3 - Trials and Temptations

"Have we trials and temptations
Is there trouble anywhere
We should never be discouraged
Take it to the Lord in prayer"

1 Corinthians 10:13 - The temptations in your life are no different from what others experience. And God is faithful. He will not allow the temptation to be more than you can stand. When you are tempted, he will show you a way out so that you can endure.

James 1:2-4 - Dear brothers and sisters, when troubles of any kind come your way, consider it an opportunity for great joy. For you know that when your faith is tested, your endurance has a chance to grow. So let it grow, for when your endurance is fully developed, you will be perfect and complete, needing nothing.

Did you know that troubles in life can actually work for your good? The writer of James is the brother of Jesus and he tells us that we should be joyful when trouble hits because it tests our faith which grows our endurance and brings spiritual maturity in our lives. It's never easy to walk through difficult times, but as we turn to God in the difficulty He actually uses it for our own good.

Temptations are a different beast altogether. They can be very destructive in our lives when left unchecked. As I talk to people, what I have learned is that no matter what age you are, temptation never goes away. It may look different in your 80s or 90s compared to your 20s or 30s, but it's still present in your life. The encouraging thing is that God always provides a way out, we just have to turn to Him to find it.

Father God - We thank you that you use things for our good even when we can't see it or understand it. We turn to you with our troubles and we ask that you help us see things from your perspective. We also turn to you with our temptations in life and ask that you would show us the way out. Thank you for your faithfulness to offer a way out every time.

In the name of Jesus, Amen.

Questions:

1. **Can you think of a time where God used a troubling situation to grow your faith?**

2. **How does temptation look different for you in this season than it did 10, 20, or even 30 years ago?**

Day 4 - The Lord is our Refuge

"Are we weak and heavy-laden
Cumbered with a load of care
Precious Savior, still our refuge
Take it to the Lord in prayer"

Psalm 91:1-2 - Whoever dwells in the shelter of the Most High will rest in the shadow of the Almighty. I will say of the Lord, "He is my refuge and my fortress, my God, in whom I trust."

Psalm 18:1-2 - I love you, Lord; you are my strength. The Lord is my rock, my fortress, and my savior; my God is my rock, in whom I find protection. He is my shield, the power that saves me, and my place of safety.

The word "refuge" in scripture means a place of safety, shelter and protection. This is what God is for us, a place where we can find safety and shelter when the storms of life hit. He is ready to help in times of trouble. He also provides the strength that we need to endure.

I love that Psalm 91 includes the concept of trust. The reason that we can find shelter and rest in God is because we trust Him to take care of us. We trust that His intentions are pure and are always in our best interest.

It can be challenging to trust God especially if we struggle to trust people, but God truly is worthy of our trust. He knows what we need even better than we do and is always motivated by love.

The best way to find shelter in God is by spending time with Him. Prayer is a huge part of connecting with Him. Another way is by spending time with people that you know have a good relationship with God. Their relationship with God pours out of them and encourages your own heart. Spending time in scripture is also essential. Scripture brings us into the truth of God's word. Another way to find refuge in God is through song. As we sing songs to God, we declare what we believe and this helps change our thinking from earthly things to heavenly things.

Father God - We thank you that you are our refuge and strength. We thank you that you are always ready to help in times of trouble. Help us remember to run to you and not try to fix things on our own.

In the name of Jesus, Amen.

Questions:

1. **We talked about a few ways to connect with God (prayer, relationships with others, reading Scripture, singing). What ways seem to work best for you?**

2. **Is there a time in life where you remember the Lord being a refuge (place of shelter and protection) for you?**

3. **How is God a refuge to you right now in your life?**

Day 5 - A Faithful Friend

*"Can we find a friend so faithful
Who will all our sorrows share
Jesus knows our every weakness
Take it to the Lord in prayer"*

Matthew 11:28 - Then Jesus said, "Come to me, all of you who are weary and carry heavy burdens, and I will give you rest."

Deuteronomy 7:9 - Understand, therefore, that the Lord your God is indeed God. He is the faithful God who keeps his covenant for a thousand generations and lavishes his unfailing love on those who love him and obey his commands.

Jesus is the type of friend who tells us to come to Him when we are weary or carrying heavy burdens and as we do that, He gives us rest. He doesn't want us to figure it out and clean ourselves up before we come to Him but to come to Him in the midst of it. He is so humble and gentle and teaches us what it means to have rest in the midst of burdens.

Burdens come in all shapes and sizes. Sometimes we are so used to carrying our burdens, along with the burdens of those around us, that we don't even think to come to God with them, but the truth is that those burdens are weighing you down. You were not meant to live with that heavy load.

You don't have to carry that load of burdens around on your shoulders. Allow God to take that load and give you the rest that you need.

Father God - Thank you for your unconditional love. Help us see the burdens that we have been carrying. We surrender these burdens to you. We thank you that you carry them for us. We receive the rest that only you can provide.

In the name of Jesus, Amen.

Questions:

1. **When a person loves deeply they tend to carry other people's burdens on their shoulders. Do you think that you do this at times?**

   a. **How can you be intentional about taking those burdens to the Lord instead of carrying them?**

2. **What are some burdens that weigh you down in your life that you need to take to the Lord?**

Week 4: Great is the Lord

SONG FOR THE WEEK - How Great Thou Art

VERSE 1:
Oh Lord, my God
When I, in awesome wonder
Consider all the worlds Thy hands have made
I see the stars, I hear the rolling thunder
Thy power throughout the universe displayed
CHORUS:
Then sings my soul, my Savior God to Thee
How great Thou art, how great Thou art
Then sings my soul, my Savior God to Thee
How great Thou art, how great Thou art
VERSE 2:
And when I think that God, His Son not sparing
Sent Him to die, I scarce can take it in
That on the cross, my burden gladly bearing
He bled and died to take away my sin
VERSE 3:
When Christ shall come, with shout of acclamation
And take me home, what joy shall fill my heart
Then I shall bow, in humble adoration
And then proclaim, my God, how great Thou art

Day 1 - Our God is Great

"Then sings my soul, My Savior God to Thee
How great Thou art, How great Thou art"

Psalm 145:2-3 - I will praise you every day; yes, I will praise you forever. Great is the Lord! He is most worthy of praise! No one can measure his greatness.

Psalm 34:1-3 - I will praise the Lord at all times. I will constantly speak his praises. I will boast only in the Lord; let all who are helpless take heart. Come, let us tell of the Lord's greatness; let us exalt his name together.

Praise is the natural response when we reflect on the greatness of God. It is hard to comprehend how great our God truly is. As we look around at the vastness of the sky or the greatness of mountains or oceans, we get filled with a glimpse of God's greatness yet we still can't fully grasp it.

As we focus on the greatness of God, the challenges we face in life get put in the proper perspective. God is always greater than anything we are up against.

No matter what kind of season of life you are in, I encourage you to reflect on the greatness of God today. Sing out His praises and let the wonder of His greatness fill your heart and soul. As we praise Him, it replaces worry and fear with awe and wonder of our God.

Father God - We praise you today and every day. You are truly great. No matter what we are facing in life we will still praise you. We recognize that you are bigger than anything that we face and are forever worthy of our praise.

In the name of Jesus, Amen.

Questions:

1. **What are some of your favorite hymns or songs of praise?**

2. **What moments in life have filled you with the most awe and wonder of God?**

Day 2 - More than we Think

1 Chronicles 29:11 - Yours, O Lord, is the greatness, the power, the glory, the victory, and the majesty. Everything in the heavens and on earth is yours, O Lord, and this is your kingdom. We adore you as the one who is over all things.

Ephesians 3:20 - Now all glory to God, who is able, through his mighty power at work within us, to accomplish infinitely more than we might ask or think.

Isaiah 55:8-9 - "For my thoughts are not your thoughts, neither are your ways my ways," declares the Lord. "As the heavens are higher than the earth, so are my ways higher than your ways and my thoughts than your thoughts."

God's ways are always higher than our ways. That means that when we can't see the solution to a problem, we can trust that God is working in ways that we would not come up with. He is truly able to accomplish infinitely more than we could ask or think.

I encourage you to think about situations or even relationships that you have given up on because you couldn't see how it would work out. Invite God into the situation. Ask for forgiveness for not trusting Him with it to begin with and then sit back and watch Him work. Don't assume that you will understand everything along the way because His ways are not your ways. He is more able than we think!

Father God - We thank you that you are so much greater than we are. We know that your thoughts and your ways are higher than ours and we ask for forgiveness for times in life when we have limited you to our own understanding. We give you every part of our life and we ask for you to do things that only you can do.

In the name of Jesus, Amen.

Questions:

1. **Are there people in your life where you desire reconciliation?**

   a. **Describe what happened in the relationship.**

   b. **Have you reached out to the person to offer reconciliation?**

   c. **Even if you think the relationship is beyond repair, I encourage you to reach out (phone, letter, face-to-face, etc.) and do what you can to offer that. You cannot control their response, that part is up to them, but you can leave this earth with the reassurance that you did your part to offer peace.**

   d. **What situation do you need to surrender to God and allow Him to work in a way that is beyond your control or understanding?**

Day 3 - The Universe Displays the Greatness of God

"Oh Lord, my God, When I, in awesome wonder
Consider all the worlds Thy hands have made
I see the stars, I hear the rolling thunder
Thy power throughout the universe displayed"

Genesis 1:1-2 - In the beginning God created the heavens and the earth. The earth was formless and empty, and darkness covered the deep waters. And the Spirit of God was hovering over the surface of the waters.

Psalm 8:3-4 When I look at the night sky and see the work of your fingers—the moon and the stars you set in place—what are mere mortals that you should think about them, human beings that you should care for them?

As we reflect on creation it bears witness to the greatness of God. In the beginning the earth was formless and empty but look at it now! That is something that only our God is capable of. It wasn't something that randomly formed itself. There is such divine craftsmanship in every detail of creation from the smallest of insects to the canvas of stars that we see in the night sky.

If you are able, I encourage you to spend some time outside today. Look around and reflect on all that you see in God's creation. As you do this you will be filled with a sense of awe and wonder. If you are not able to physically go outside, close your eyes and think about your favorite parts of nature. Creation truly testifies to how great our God is.

Father God - We thank you for the beautiful creation all around us. We pray that we would slow down more often to recognize your handiwork that is all around us. You are the creator of the heavens and the earth and we worship you!

In the name of Jesus, Amen.

Questions:

1. **What part of creation fills you the most with a sense of God's greatness and power?**

2. **What are some of your favorite ways to enjoy God's creation?**

Day 4 - His Son not Sparing

"And when I think that God, His Son not sparing
Sent Him to die, I scarce can take it in
That on the cross, my burden gladly bearing
He bled and died to take away my sin"

1 John 4:9-10 - God showed how much he loved us by sending his one and only Son into the world so that we might have eternal life through him. This is real love—not that we loved God, but that he loved us and sent his Son as a sacrifice to take away our sins.

1 John 3:16 - We know what real love is because Jesus gave up his life for us. So we also ought to give up our lives for our brothers and sisters.

One thing that has always amazed me about God is not only is He incredibly great and powerful, but He is also incredibly loving. In fact, that is who God is, in one word He is love (1 John 4:16). Love is what motivated Him to send His only Son as a sacrifice to take away our sins.

The love of God should motivate us to love others. Because Jesus gave up His life for us, we also ought to give up our lives for those around us. It is so easy to focus on ourselves each day. Looking out for ourselves comes natural to us, but that is not what God has called us to do.

Be intentional today to look for opportunities to serve those around you. It doesn't have to be something elaborate. It can be as simple as greeting someone with a smile or saying thank you. God will direct you and show you how to love those He puts in front of you, all you need to do is say yes.

Father God - As we reflect on your love the words 'thank you' are not enough. Your love is deeper than any love we have ever known. We pray that as we receive your love today, that it would motivate us to extend that love to those around us. Show us how you want us to love those around us today.

In the name of Jesus, Amen.

Questions:

1. **What are some simple ways that you can show love to those around you?**

2. **What are some of the ways you sense God's love in your life right now?**

3. **When did you first sense the love of God in your life?**

Day 5 - Homecoming

"When Christ shall come, with shout of acclamation
And take me home, what joy shall fill my heart
Then I shall bow, in humble adoration
And then proclaim, my God, how great Thou art"

John 14:1-4 - Don't let your hearts be troubled. Trust in God, and trust also in me. There is more than enough room in my Father's home. If this were not so, would I have told you that I am going to prepare a place for you? When everything is ready, I will come and get you, so that you will always be with me where I am. And you know the way to where I am going.

Philippians 3:20-21 - But we are citizens of heaven, where the Lord Jesus Christ lives. And we are eagerly waiting for him to return as our Savior. He will take our weak mortal bodies and change them into glorious bodies like his own, using the same power with which he will bring everything under his control.

We should live eagerly awaiting for Jesus to return as our Savior as we anticipate spending all of eternity with Him. What a glorious day that will be! It is so encouraging to think about how Jesus is preparing a place for us even now and that He will come to get us when everything is ready.

Did you realize that you get a new body? Jesus takes our weak mortal bodies and changes them into glorious bodies like His own. That alone is reason to celebrate!

Our minds cannot comprehend all of eternity, but we know that it is going to be amazing and glorious to be face-to-face with our Savior. Spend time today reflecting on the truth that this is not your permanent home. Allow excitement and anticipation to flood your heart as you reflect on the things of eternity.

Father God - We know that this is not our permanent home. We are citizens of heaven. Help us to live lives that glorify you and shine your light to those around us so that they too would be drawn to you. Flood us with anticipation for the things of eternity today!

In the name of Jesus, Amen.

Questions:

1. **Have you spent much time pondering the things of eternity?**

2. **What comes to mind when you think about heaven?**

3. **What areas of your body give you the most trouble?**

    a. **Does it excite you that you get a new body?**

Week 5: It is Well

SONG FOR THE WEEK - It Is Well With My Soul

VERSE 1:
When peace like a river attendeth my way
When sorrows like sea billows roll
Whatever my lot, Thou hast taught me to say
It is well, it is well with my soul
CHORUS:
It is well
With my soul
It is well, it is well with my soul
VERSE 2:
Though Satan should buffet, though trials should come
Let this blest assurance control
That Christ has regarded my helpless estate
And has shed His own blood for my soul
VERSE 3:
My sin, oh the bliss of this glorious thought
My sin, not in part, but the whole
Is nailed to the cross, and I bear it no more
Praise the Lord, praise the Lord, O my soul
VERSE 4:
And Lord, haste the day when my faith shall be sight
The clouds be rolled back as a scroll
The trump shall resound, and the Lord shall descend
Even so, it is well with my soul

Day 1 - Whatever my lot

"When peace like a river attendeth my way
When sorrows like sea billows roll
Whatever my lot, Thou hast taught me to say
It is well, it is well with my soul"

Isaiah 43:2 - When you go through deep waters, I will be with you.
When you go through rivers of difficulty, you will not drown. When
you walk through the fire of oppression, you will not be burned up;
the flames will not consume you.

Philippians 4:12-13 - I know how to live on almost nothing or with
everything. I have learned the secret of living in every situation,
whether it is with a full stomach or empty, with plenty or little. For I
can do everything through Christ, who gives me strength.

The song "It Is Well With My Soul" is a favorite hymn for many but
not all know the story behind this song. A woman named Anna and
her four daughters were aboard a ship and were crossing the Atlantic
Ocean in 1873. About four days into the trip their ship collided with
another ship leaving all the passengers in the ocean.

A sailor that was rowing a small boat spotted Anna floating on a
piece of the ship. Sadly, Anna's daughters did not survive. The sailor
pulled Anna onto his boat and they boarded a larger ship from there.

Anna's husband, Horatio Spafford, was devastated to learn that his
four daughters had drowned. He immediately boarded a ship to

reunite with his wife. As he came through the spot where his daughters had drowned the captain notified him, and it was in that place that Horatio began to pen the song, "It Is Well With My Soul."

What incredible faith this man had in the Lord to be able to rest in God's peace even in such a devastating time in his life. He was in a place where he knew how to reach out to his Heavenly Father no matter what was taking place around him.

Father God - We thank you that no matter what we go through in life that you are there in the midst of it all. We thank you for the strength that you give to us for each season of life. Help us to turn to you in times of difficulty and to sense your hand that is always with us.

In the name of Jesus, Amen.

Questions:

1. **Have you had a time in life where you dealt with tremendous loss?**

2. **Looking back can you see how God's hand was with you?**

Day 2 - My Sin was Nailed to the Cross

"My sin, oh the bliss of this glorious thought
My sin, not in part, but the whole
Is nailed to the cross, and I bear it no more
Praise the Lord, praise the Lord, O my soul"

Psalm 103:10-12 - He does not punish us for all our sins; he does not deal harshly with us, as we deserve. For his unfailing love toward those who fear him is as great as the height of the heavens above the earth. He has removed our sins as far from us as the east is from the west.

Hebrews 10:12 - But our High Priest offered himself to God as a single sacrifice for sins, good for all time. Then he sat down in the place of honor at God's right hand.

The verse of the hymn "It Is Well With My Soul" that says, "My sin not in part but the whole is nailed to the cross and I bear it no more. Praise the Lord, praise the Lord O my soul" always causes intense gratitude to bubble up within me. I love the emphasis on our *entire sin* being forgiven. The sacrifice of Jesus on the cross didn't cover only certain sin but all sin and for all time.

I also love that the lyric says "and I bear it [sin] no more." God has truly removed our sins from us as far as the east is from the west. This means that we no longer have to carry the weight of our sin. We no longer have to walk around feeling shameful or condemned for our sins. Romans 8:1 tells us that "There is no condemnation for those who belong to Christ Jesus. And because you belong to him, the power of the life-giving Spirit has freed you from the power of sin that leads to death." We have freedom in Christ from sin and the condemnation that it brings! This ought to cause us to praise like the song says.

Some of you have done things in your life that you regret and you have never told anyone. You have carried the weight of those things for many years. It is time to let go of that weight. Confess the sin to God and then receive the forgiveness that He offers. You don't need to carry that load anymore!

Father God - We thank you for the forgiveness we have through Jesus. We couldn't earn forgiveness or be strong enough to defeat sin in our lives so we thank you that you made a way for us. Help us to release all shame in our hearts and walk in total freedom from sin and condemnation.

In the name of Jesus, Amen.

Questions:

1. **When did you first experience the forgiveness of sin?**

2. **Have you dealt with shame or condemnation in your life?**

Day 3 - When My Faith Shall be Sight

"And Lord, haste the day when my faith shall be sight
The clouds be rolled back as a scroll
The trump shall resound, and the Lord shall descend
Even so, it is well with my soul"

Matthew 26:64 - Jesus replied, "You have said it. And in the future you will see the Son of Man seated in the place of power at God's right hand and coming on the clouds of heaven."

1 Thessalonians 4:16-18 - For the Lord himself will come down from heaven with a commanding shout, with the voice of the archangel, and with the trumpet call of God. First, the believers who have died will rise from their graves. Then, together with them, we who are still alive and remain on the earth will be caught up in the clouds to meet the Lord in the air. Then we will be with the Lord forever. So encourage each other with these words.

The writer of "It Is Well With My Soul" references the day that these scriptures talk about. We barely can comprehend what it will be like when the Lord returns, but we can be certain that we will be with the Lord which is why the lyric says, "Even so, it is well with my soul."

The things of eternity do not need to be feared. Questions like "did I do enough good things" or "was I a good enough person" aren't really what gets you into heaven. What opens the door of heaven for us is what Jesus did on the cross and how He rose from the dead.

As we rest in the knowledge of what Christ did on our behalf, we can look forward to the things of eternity and to the day when our "faith shall be sight."

Father God - We may not know what heaven will be like entirely or understand what the day will be like when you return to earth, but we can rest assured that we will be with you so all will be well. Help us to prepare our hearts for that day.

In the name of Jesus, Amen.

Questions:

1. **What parts of your walk with God are by faith (things that you cannot see now but someday)?**

2. **What have you been taught about the return (or second coming) of Jesus?**

Day 4 - God is Our Refuge and Strength

Psalm 46:1-2 - God is our refuge and strength, always ready to help in times of trouble. So we will not fear when earthquakes come and the mountains crumble into the sea.

Matthew 6:34 - So don't worry about tomorrow, for tomorrow will bring its own worries. Today's trouble is enough for today.

The word David used in Psalm 46 to describe God is our *refuge*. This word portrays the image of a shelter from a storm. Imagine that you are outside and all at once it starts pouring rain. Your reaction would be to take shelter inside immediately. This is what God is for us when the storms of life hit. When we are hit with things unexpectedly, we should run to the Lord for shelter.

The other word that David used is *strength*. When things hit us in life, we typically don't feel strong but instead we feel weak. It is in those moments that we can rely on the strength of God rather than our own. I love how David wrote that our God is "always ready to help in times of trouble." Our problems may take us by surprise, but God is not surprised and He is always ready to help.

It is because we know that God is on our side that we will not fear the unknown. For those of you that are trying to anticipate what tomorrow holds or even what this following year looks like, I encourage you to surrender those things to God. Trust that He is with you and is always ready to help you. Remember, He is a shelter in times of trouble and the true source of strength for you.

Father God - We thank you that you are always ready to help us in times of trouble. We surrender the worries we have to you and we ask for your strength. Help us to remember to run to you in times of need. You are the best shelter that we could ask for.

In the name of Jesus, Amen.

Questions:

1. **Have you ever been caught in a bad storm outside? What did you do to feel safe?**

2. **What does it look like to run to God for shelter when facing your storms of life?**

Day 5 - Be Strong and Courageous

Joshua 1:9 - This is my command—be strong and courageous! Do not be afraid or discouraged. For the Lord your God is with you wherever you go.

1 Peter 5:10 - So after you have suffered a little while, he will restore, support, and strengthen you, and he will place you on a firm foundation.

I love how the word courage is inside the word discouraged. When we feel discouraged about something, it robs us of the courage that we need to face the situation. As a hospice chaplain, I often talk to people who feel afraid of the future. Their courage has been removed and they need courage to face what is ahead.

The reason that we can have courage in the midst of the unknown is because we know the Lord will always be with us. That is what I want to remind you of today. No matter what is ahead of you, God will be with you, so you do not need to be afraid or discouraged.

After you have suffered a little while our God will restore, support, and strengthen you. He will place you on a firm foundation (1 Peter 5:10). As hard as it is right now, the suffering won't last forever.

Take courage today, no matter what you are up against, and remember that the Lord is with you.

Father God - We thank you that you are always with us and because you are with us we can take courage. We do not need to fear the unknown but instead we can trust that you are in control. We thank you that suffering does not last forever and that you even use it to make us more like you and draw us closer to yourself.

In the name of Jesus, Amen.

Questions:

1. **What are the things in life right now that are discouraging for you?**

   a. **How can knowing that God is with you help you replace your discouragement with courage?**

2. **What is a time in your life when God has taken something difficult and turned it into something good?**

Week 6: All to Him I Owe

SONG FOR THE WEEK - Jesus Paid it All

VERSE 1:
I hear the Savior say
Thy strength indeed is small
Child of weakness, watch and pray
Find in Me thine all in all
CHORUS:
Jesus paid it all
All to Him I owe
Sin had left a crimson stain
He washed it white as snow
VERSE 2:
And now complete in Him
My robe, His righteousness
Close sheltered 'neath His side
I am divinely blest
VERSE 3:
Lord, now indeed I find
Thy pow'r, and Thine alone
Can change the leper's spots
And melt the heart of stone
VERSE 4:
When from my dying bed
My ransomed soul shall rise
"Jesus died my soul to save"
Shall rend the vaulted skies
VERSE 5 :
And when before the throne
I stand in Him complete
I'll lay my trophies down
All down at Jesus' feet

Day 1 - Child of Weakness

"I hear the Savior say
Thy strength indeed is small
Child of weakness, watch and pray
Find in Me thine all in all"

Isaiah 40:28-29 - Do you not know? Have you not heard? The Lord is the everlasting God, the Creator of the ends of the earth. He will not grow tired or weary, and his understanding no one can fathom. He gives strength to the weary and increases the power of the weak.

1 Chronicles 16:11 - Search for the Lord and for his strength; continually seek him.

The reality is that at times we feel weak. We may not always admit it, but deep down we aren't always sure how we are going to make it through. The good news is that God knows we are weak in those areas and He offers His strength to get us through.

Some of us may feel weak physically. Things that we used to be able to do with ease are much more difficult now. Some of us might feel weak mentally or emotionally as we face situations that are too big for us to solve. Some of us may feel weak spiritually as we undergo spiritual attack or are feeling weary in our faith.

No matter what type of weakness we face God meets us in it. The key to finding God's strength is to seek Him continually. Spending time in God's presence doing things like praying, reading the Bible, singing praises to God, having conversations with others about your faith are all ways to seek God and in doing so be filled with His strength.

Father God - We admit that we feel weak at times and we thank you that you offer us your strength. Our desire is to be with you at all times. Help us to be more aware of your presence in our lives. We receive your strength today.

In the name of Jesus, Amen.

Questions:

1. **In what way do you feel weak right now?**

2. **What is your favorite way to spend time with God?**

Day 2 - Robe of Righteousness

"And now complete in Him
My robe, His righteousness
Close sheltered 'neath His side
I am divinely blest"

Isaiah 61:10 - I am overwhelmed with joy in the Lord my God! For he has dressed me with the clothing of salvation and draped me in a robe of righteousness. I am like a bridegroom dressed for his wedding or a bride with her jewels.

Matthew 22:11-13 - But when the king came in to meet the guests, he noticed a man who wasn't wearing the proper clothes for a wedding. 'Friend,' he asked, 'how is it that you are here without wedding clothes?' But the man had no reply. Then the king said to his aides, 'Bind his hands and feet and throw him into the outer darkness, where there will be weeping and gnashing of teeth.'

The parable that Jesus shared in Matthew 22 is about the Kingdom of Heaven. Jesus used an illustration of a king who invited people to a wedding celebration for his son. His first list of invited guests all refused to come! The king decided to invite everyone to the celebration, not just those on the original list. The banquet hall filled up quickly with guests. This represents God opening the invitation of salvation to all people rather than a select few.

While they are at the wedding the king notices a man not wearing the proper clothes and his reaction seems a little harsh until we understand the context of a wedding in this culture. The man has no response as to why he wasn't wearing the proper clothing so he is thrown into the outer darkness.

At first glance it seems like the punishment doesn't fit the crime, but in this culture all of the guests would have been given wedding clothes to wear at the wedding. So to see someone not wearing the clothes provided was essentially rejecting the clothing offered in order to be appropriately dressed for the occasion.

In the same way, God doesn't expect us to show up to the Kingdom of Heaven and be able to afford what is needed to get in. He provides it for us. He purchased what was needed through His son and it is freely offered to everyone. We must choose to put on the righteousness that was purchased on the cross rather than thinking we can somehow attain it on our own.

Father God - We thank you that you clothe us in righteousness through Jesus. Help us to see the areas where we are still trying to earn our way to heaven rather than accepting the gift that is freely given to us.

In the name of Jesus, Amen.

Questions:

1. **What is the best wedding (or any) celebration you've ever attended?**

2. **How does it make you feel to know that righteousness isn't something you work for but instead something that you receive?**

Day 3 - Thy Power Alone

"Lord, now indeed I find
Thy pow'r, and Thine alone
Can change the leper's spots
And melt the heart of stone"

Matthew 8:1-3 - Large crowds followed Jesus as he came down the mountainside. Suddenly, a man with leprosy approached him and knelt before him. "Lord," the man said, "if you are willing, you can heal me and make me clean." Jesus reached out and touched him. "I am willing," he said. "Be healed!" And instantly the leprosy disappeared.

Ezekiel 36:26 - And I will give you a new heart, and I will put a new spirit in you. I will take out your stony, stubborn heart and give you a tender, responsive heart.

It is so important for us to recognize the power of God. His power is unlike any other power. He is the only one that can truly heal a person and the only one that can soften a heart of stone.

If we don't recognize the power of God, we will go to other sources for help in times of need. We serve an amazing God. I love the passage we read above where Jesus healed a man with leprosy. The man approached Jesus and said, "If you are willing you can heal me..." Jesus responded saying, "I am willing" and the man was healed.

Sometimes we don't recognize how willing God is to intervene in our lives. Take some time today to think about what area you need healing in. It could be physical healing but it could also be healing spiritually or emotionally from wounds that you have acquired over the years.

Father God - We recognize that you alone have the power to heal. We ask that you would soften the areas in our hearts that have become hard. We also ask you to show us the places where we need healing and send your healing power into those places. Thank you for your willingness to heal!

In the name of Jesus, Amen.

Questions:

1. **In what ways have you seen the healing power of God in your life?**

2. **Are there areas (physical, mental, emotional, spiritual) where you need God's healing?**

3. **Have you seen God melt a person's heart of stone? Explain.**

Day 4 - From My Dying Bed

"When from my dying bed
My ransomed soul shall rise
'Jesus died my soul to save'
Shall rend the vaulted skies"

Psalm 23:1-4 - The Lord is my shepherd; I shall not want. He makes me to lie down in green pastures; He leads me beside the still waters. He restores my soul; He leads me in the paths of righteousness; For His name's sake. Yea, though I walk through the valley of the shadow of death, I will fear no evil;

For You are with me; Your rod and Your staff, they comfort me.

John 11:25 - Jesus told her, "I am the resurrection and the life. Anyone who believes in me will live, even after dying.

Even as we walk through the valley of the shadow of death we do not have to fear because we know the one who is with us. God brings us comfort even in our most challenging moments. God will lead you beside still waters in your heart and He will restore your soul. He also leads us in the paths of righteousness. God's role is to lead and your role is to follow.

The reason that we don't need to fear evil is because we are certain that God is with us. I hope that you have that assurance today in your heart that God is with you. If you can't say that for certain, I encourage you to take some time and invite God into your heart and your situation. Ask Him to bring you the comfort that you need.

Jesus tells us that He is the resurrection and the life. He conquered even death itself when He rose from the dead. He promises that anyone who believes in Him will live even after dying. My hope is that this brings you great comfort and peace today. This is not the end, it is just the beginning.

Father God - There is nothing more final on earth than death. Help us to have peace and joy knowing that you made a way for us to live even after we die. Give us assurance today that you are with us and will continue to be with us as we transition from this life to the next life.

In the name of Jesus, Amen.

Questions:

1. **Do you feel ready for heaven?**

2. **Are there things you want to do before going to heaven?** *(Conversations with loved ones, forgiving people that have hurt you or those you love, seeing a special place one last time, seeing someone that you haven't seen in a while, etc.)*

Day 5 - I Stand in Him Complete

"And when before the throne
I stand in Him complete
I'll lay my trophies down
All down at Jesus' feet"

Philippians 3:8 - Yes, everything else is worthless when compared with the infinite value of knowing Christ Jesus my Lord. For his sake I have discarded everything else, counting it all as garbage, so that I could gain Christ.

Matthew 25:31-32 - When the Son of Man comes in his glory, and all the angels with him, he will sit on his glorious throne. All the nations will be gathered before him, and he will separate the people one from another as a shepherd separates the sheep from the goats.

Paul, the writer of the letter to the Philippians, says that everything is worthless when compared to knowing Christ Jesus his Lord. He didn't say compared to the knowledge of Christ Jesus. He said compared to knowing Christ Jesus. There is such a difference in knowing about Jesus and actually knowing Jesus. God truly is after a relationship with us and not a religious obligation from us.

We get trapped when we focus on the accomplishments of this life. Paul recognized that trap and said he counts everything else as garbage so that he could "gain" Christ.

The word "gain" that Paul used depicts the idea of trading something. So Paul is saying that he traded the things that were valuable in this world for Christ. He did this because he had perspective of what really matters at the end of our lives. It isn't how much we have accomplished or how much we have acquired. At the end of it all, what matters most is our relationship with Christ and how we brought those around us into that same relationship.

Father God - We thank you for your son, Jesus. Nothing that this world offers compares to Him. Show us the areas where things of this world are fighting for our affections. We want to trade all the things of this world so that we gain Christ Jesus our Lord.

In the name of Jesus, Amen.

Questions:

1. **What are some of the things that you value the most in this life?**

2. **Would you say you were taught to know Jesus or more to just attend church and know about Jesus?**

    a. **How are the two different?**

    b. **How can you move closer to knowing Jesus?**

Week 7: Our Father's World

SONG FOR THE WEEK - This is My Father's World

VERSE 1:
This is my Father's world
And to my listening ears
All nature sings, and round me rings
The music of the spheres
This is my Father's world
I rest me in the thought
Of rocks and trees, of skies and seas
His hand the wonders wrought
VERSE 2:
This is my Father's world
The birds their carols raise
The morning light, the lily white
Declare their maker's praise
This is my Father's world
He shines in all that's fair
In the rustling grass I hear Him pass
He speaks to me everywhere
VERSE 3:
This is my Father's world
O let me ne'er forget
That though the wrong seems oft so strong
God is the ruler yet
This is my Father's world
why should my heart be sad
The Lord is King; let the heavens ring
God reigns; let the earth be glad

Day 1 - Rest for Your Soul

"This is my Father's world
I rest me in the thought
Of rocks and trees, of skies and seas
His hand the wonders wrought"

Matthew 11:28-29 - Come to me, all you who are weary and burdened, and I will give you rest. Take my yoke upon you and learn from me, for I am gentle and humble in heart, and you will find rest for your souls.

Psalm 4:8 - In peace I will lie down and sleep, for you alone, O Lord, will keep me safe.

Some days we just need rest. Real soul level rest. We aren't talking about a good nap. This is a kind of rest that is only found in God. Jesus has an open invitation to come to Him when we are weary and He says that He will give us rest.

We live in such a fast paced world that at times we can feel guilty that we need to rest, but rest is something that God designed us to need. We are created in the image of God and even He rested according to Genesis 2.

Allow yourself space to find rest and as you rest, lean into the presence of God. Let His peace and love wash over you. Don't allow guilt or busyness to crowd your mind but, instead, enjoy and receive God's rest for you.

Father God - We thank you that you are a God who modeled what it means to rest. Rest is truly a holy time with you. Help us to come to Jesus when we are weary instead of trying to just keep going forward and overworking ourselves. We receive your rest today.

In the name of Jesus, Amen.

Questions:

1. **Have you felt weary lately and in need of rest? If so, in what areas do you feel weary?**

2. **Do you ever struggle feeling guilty that you need to rest? Do you feel like you should be doing more?**

3. **Knowing God made us to need rest, how can you create restful times for yourself?**

Day 2 - The Maker's Praise

"This is my Father's world
The birds their carols raise
The morning light, the lily white
Declare their maker's praise"

Psalm 104:24 - O Lord, what a variety of things you have made! In wisdom you have made them all. The earth is full of your creatures.

Isaiah 40:26 - Look up into the heavens. Who created all the stars? He brings them out like an army, one after another, calling each by its name. Because of his great power and incomparable strength, not a single one is missing.

We serve a creative God! When I look at His creation, I am blown away by the details God put into it. Butterflies and their specific and intricate designs, flowers and the variety of colors that they display, birds and the array of sounds that they make as well as their incredibly vibrant colors all point to the creativity of God.

When we take time to really notice God's creation, it fills us with awe and wonder. He has power and strength like no one else. I love the verse in this song as it says, "the birds their carols raise, the morning light, the lily white declare their maker's praise." The idea that as creation simply exists (birds singing, lilies displaying their color, the sun rising beautifully) it declares the praise of their maker.

I wonder if God made creation so beautiful so that we would have something incredible to enjoy. We have so many distractions in life that often we don't even take time to enjoy the creation that is all around us, let alone allow it to connect us to our creator. Let's take time every day to enjoy the beauty that God has created.

Father God - We join in with creation today and we give praise to our maker. We know that you are a creator God and we stand in awe of you today. Help us to notice the creation that is all around us.

In the name of Jesus, Amen.

Questions:

1. **What is a detail in creation that you have to slow down to notice?** (dainty wings of a hummingbird, varieties in color of a butterfly, shapes of the clouds, etc.)

2. **What are some distractions in life that keep you from noticing God's creation?**

Day 3 - He Speaks to Me

"This is my Father's world
He shines in all that's fair
In the rustling grass I hear Him pass
He speaks to me everywhere"

John 10:27-28 - My sheep listen to my voice; I know them, and they follow me. I give them eternal life, and they will never perish. No one can snatch them away from me.

Psalm 16:11 - You will show me the way of life, granting me the joy of your presence and the pleasures of living with you forever.

God desires us to hear His voice, but we have to posture our hearts in a way to hear His voice. The author of this song understood that he could hear the voice of God everywhere. It is about having a continual walk with God, not moments here and there where we make time to pray.

As we open ourselves up to see God and to hear from Him, we can have fellowship with Him at all times. While we are resting or working, while we are folding laundry or doing dishes, while we are sitting quietly or having conversations, we can have fellowship with our Lord in it all.

When we learn to live in the presence of God, there is so much joy in our lives. It isn't a joy that comes and goes with the ups and downs of life, but a steady joy that is present because of the one who is with us. This type of joy is visible to those around you and will draw them into the presence of God as well.

Father God - Thank you for your presence and for speaking to us. Help us to understand that you desire a constant fellowship with us. Help us to learn to connect with you continually and to see you in even the small things. We want to carry your joy and your presence to those around us.

In the name of Jesus, Amen.

Questions:

1. **Do you sense that God is always with you?**

2. **How do you experience His presence?**

3. **Describe a time where you heard from God.** (This doesn't have to be an audible voice. It could be a time where you sensed His voice in your heart.)

Day 4 - God is the Ruler Yet

"This is my Father's world
O let me ne'er forget
That though the wrong seems oft so strong
God is the ruler yet"

2 Chronicles 7:14 - Then if my people who are called by my name will humble themselves and pray and seek my face and turn from their wicked ways, I will hear from heaven and will forgive their sins and restore their land.

Psalm 22:28 - For royal power belongs to the Lord. He rules all the nations.

The third verse of this song brings me so much comfort. It's the idea that even though evil seems to prevail in this world and people that are doing wrong seem to succeed, God is still on the throne and in control. One of my patients was typically depressed when I would come for a visit and it never failed that he would be watching the news (all day, every day). I am not saying that we should be uninformed, but if you continually view all the wrong that is in the world, it leads to a pretty depressing frame of mind.

We can rest in the truth that even though things seem like they are backwards in this world, God has the final victory and therefore so do we! He truly does rule all the nations whether they know it or not.

What is our part in this fallen world? Our part is to humble ourselves, pray, seek God's face and to turn from any wickedness in our lives.

When we do this, God says that He hears us from heaven, forgives our sins and **restores our land.**

We live in a world that is in need of restoration. Our world needs people who are willing to humble themselves and pray in order for the restoration of God to come.

Let's not get discouraged with the condition of the world around us but, instead, let's keep in mind that God is the true ruler and that we can make real change as we cry out to Him.

Father God - We recognize that you are the true ruler of the world. We humble ourselves before you and repent of all sin in our lives. We ask that you would restore our nation and our world to be a people that worship the one true God.

In the name of Jesus, Amen.

Questions:

1. **Do you get discouraged at the condition of our world and society?**

2. **How does it bring comfort to you to recognize that God is ultimately in control of this world?**

3. **What specifically do you feel God calling you to pray about for our world?**

Day 5 - Let the Earth be Glad

"This is my Father's world
why should my heart be sad
The Lord is King; let the heavens ring
God reigns; let the earth be glad"

Psalm 100:2 - Worship the Lord with gladness. Come before him, singing with joy.

Acts 2:46 - They worshiped together at the Temple each day, met in homes for the Lord's Supper, and shared their meals with great joy and generosity.

Knowing that this is our Father's world should fill us with joy and gladness. David wrote in Psalm 100 that we should come before God singing with joy. Joy doesn't always come automatically. Sometimes we have to make the decision to put on joy, and one great way to do that is through singing His praises. That's why we have a designated hymn for each week in this devotional. As we sing the truth of the lyrics, it fills our hearts with joy and connects us to God.

Another great way to find real joy is with the fellowship of other Christians. God designed us to live in relationship with other people. He didn't intend for us to live in isolation. We need other people to encourage us and motivate us to live lives that honor God. As we spend time with other Christians, it fills our hearts with joy.

It can be easy to isolate ourselves or think that we really don't need people. Sometimes we do this because we have been hurt by people.

Sometimes we do this because the people that used to be in our lives are gone and we don't know how to replace them. Ask God to show you who He has provided in your life in order for you to have the kind of relationships that give you joy.

Father God - We thank you for the joy that comes from you. We worship you today! We praise you and receive your joy today. Show us who you are asking us to build relationships with both for our benefit and for their benefit.

In the name of Jesus, Amen.

Questions:

1. **What are some of your favorite hymns or songs to sing to God?**

2. **Friendship is so important. Who was your closest friend in:**

   a. **Childhood?**

   b. **Young adult life?**

   c. **Later adult life?**

Week 8: Jesus is Calling

SONG FOR THE WEEK - Softly and Tenderly

VERSE 1:
Softly and tenderly Jesus is calling
Calling for you and for me
See on the portals He's waiting and watching
Watching for you and for me
CHORUS:
Come home, come home
Ye who are weary, come home
Earnestly, tenderly, Jesus is calling
Calling, O sinner, come home
VERSE 2:
Why should we tarry when Jesus is pleading
Pleading for you and for me
Why should we linger and heed not His mercies
Mercies for you and for me
VERSE 3:
O for the wonderful love He has promised
Promised for you and for me
Though we have sinned, He has mercy and pardon
Pardon for you and for me

Day 1 - Come Home

"Come home, come home
Ye who are weary, come home
Earnestly, tenderly, Jesus is calling
Calling, O sinner, come home"

Luke 15:20 - So he got up and went to his father. "But while he was still a long way off, his father saw him and was filled with compassion for him; he ran to his son, threw his arms around him and kissed him.

Psalm 139:23-24 - Search me, God, and know my heart; test me and know my anxious thoughts. See if there is any offensive way in me, and lead me in the way everlasting.

Whenever I sing the song "Softly and Tenderly," I am reminded of the parable of the prodigal son that Jesus talks about in Luke 15. A man had two sons. One day the younger son asked his father for his share of the estate. After he had received it he moved away and spent all the money on wild living. Eventually he ran out of money and a famine hit the land so he tried to find work in order to survive. The Bible says that he "came to his senses" and decided to return to his father's house and offer himself as a servant.

While the son was still a long way away his father saw him and was **filled with compassion for him** and ran to his son. The son told his father that he wasn't worthy of being called a son. The father's response was to throw a huge party in celebration of his son's return home.

This is a picture of the heart of God towards us. Whether we turned away from God in a major way or we turned away from Him in a small area of our heart, He is ready to welcome us home. He has compassion for us so we do not need to fear returning to God.

I encourage you to examine your heart today. Ask God to search your heart and to show you if there is anything in you that is not pleasing to Him. It is never too late to turn back to God. Don't let fear or pride stand in your way. He is waiting for you with open arms.

Father God - We thank you that you are a God that is full of compassion. We don't have to fear coming back to you because we know that your love for us is unconditional. We ask that you examine our hearts and show us anything that is not pleasing to you. Father, lead us on the path of everlasting life.

In the name of Jesus, Amen.

Questions:

1. **Have you ever wandered in your faith?**

2. **How does it feel different for you when you are walking close with God compared to walking far from God?**

Day 2 - Ye Who are Weary

Matthew 11:28-29 - Come to me, all you who are weary and burdened, and I will give you rest. Take my yoke upon you and learn from me, for I am gentle and humble in heart, and you will find rest for your souls.

Isaiah 40:28-29 - Do you not know? Have you not heard? The Lord is the everlasting God, the Creator of the ends of the earth. He will not grow tired or weary, and his understanding no one can fathom. He gives strength to the weary and increases the power of the weak.

The song "Softly and Tenderly" says, "Ye who are weary, come home." When we stay disconnected from our Heavenly Father it takes a toll on our soul. We end up feeling weary and worn out. That's why Jesus gives an invitation in Matthew chapter 11 and tells us to come to Him and promises that He will give us rest. He also teaches us that He is gentle and humble at heart, and in Him we find rest for our souls.

It can be hard to admit that we need help. It can also be hard to admit or show weakness. Even if it is difficult for you to share this with people, I encourage you today to start with God. Go to Him with your burdens. If you don't know what to pray, just tell Him that you are tired and weary and need His rest.

In addition to physical rest, this hymn also references a final rest. This is where we give up our spirit and go home to be at rest with our Lord. This day may be very close for you or very far off. Eventually we all will be there, and I want to encourage you not to fight going home when your time comes. He sits and waits on the portal of heaven and calls us home. We can choose to cling to life out of fear or uncertainty, or we can trust that God will take care of what needs to be done on earth and release ourselves to our final resting place with Him. It is much more peaceful when we choose to trust God.

Father God - Although it is hard at times to admit this to people, we admit to you that we feel weary and burdened some days. We thank you for the invitation to come to you with those burdens. We also thank you for the invitation to come home. When our final days come, help us to fully trust you as we release ourselves into your hands.

In the name of Jesus, Amen.

Questions:

1. **Is it hard for you to admit when you feel weak or that you need help?**

   a. **If so, how has this affected your relationship with God?**

   b. **If not, who do you talk to when you are feeling burdened or worn out?**

2. **When you think about the day when God calls you, home do you feel uneasy or peaceful?**

Day 3 - Softly and Tenderly

"Softly and tenderly Jesus is calling
Calling for you and for me
See on the portals He's waiting and watching
Watching for you and for me"

Romans 2:4 - Or do you show contempt for the riches of his kindness, forbearance and patience, not realizing that God's kindness is intended to lead you to repentance?

Joel 2:13 - Rend your heart and not your garments. Return to the Lord your God, for he is gracious and compassionate, slow to anger and abounding in love, and he relents from sending calamity.

Our God is patient and kind. He isn't pushy and doesn't force Himself on us. However, we need to understand that His kindness is intended to lead us to a place of repentance. We should not mistake His kindness to mean that He doesn't care about how we live our lives. He desires that we return to Him with our entire heart and live, but He leaves the choice in our hands.

Our God is so beautiful. He is gracious and compassionate, slow to anger and abounding in love. He could send disaster to get our attention but, instead, He speaks quietly and waits patiently. Like our hymn for this week says, He calls us softly and tenderly not harshly and forcefully. He is waiting and watching for you and for me.

Know that God is always with you. He sees you and hasn't forgotten you, but He wants you to come to Him. He is a God who desires to be loved and that requires action on our end. Just like He pursues us, we need to pursue Him.

If you are able, I encourage you to read or listen to the Bible each day. This will draw you close to Him. I also encourage you to pray every day. This will connect you to the presence of God. Lastly, find people that you can talk about your faith with. This will connect you to the heart of God.

Father God - We thank you that you are patient, kind, gracious, compassionate, slow to anger and abounding in love. We want to come to you. Forgive us for the times when we have stayed at a distance. We want to draw close to you with all that we are.

In the name of Jesus, Amen.

Questions:

1. **Who is someone in your life that you enjoy talking to about your faith?**

2. **How have you experienced the kindness of God in your life lately or over the years?**

Day 4 - Mercy for You and for Me

"Why should we tarry when Jesus is pleading
Pleading for you and for me
Why should we linger and heed not His mercies
Mercies for you and for me"

Micah 7:18 - Who is a God like you, who pardons sin and forgives the transgression of the remnant of his inheritance? You do not stay angry forever but delight to show mercy.

Proverbs 28:13 - Whoever conceals their sins does not prosper, but the one who confesses and renounces them finds mercy.

I am so thankful that God delights to show mercy. He is a God of justice yet He delights in showing mercy. The key to unlocking mercy in our lives includes three important things:

1) Choosing not to conceal sin - the word conceal speaks to the idea of hiding or covering something up. It is like putting on a mask in front of others and doing everything you can to make sure they don't discover the sin in your life.

2) Confessing our sin - This is easier said than done for a lot of us. We know that the Bible tells us to confess our sin but it is hard to actually do it. It requires that we swallow our pride. It also requires that we extend trust to someone as we let them in on the very thing we work so hard to cover up.

3) Renouncing our sin - To renounce means to leave or forsake something. When it comes to sin, it isn't enough just to confess it

- we must leave it. That means getting rid of everything that caters to or encourages this sin in our lives. We must be willing to do whatever it takes to leave the sin.

When we are willing to do all these things, we find the mercy of God. Mercy is available to all of us and God actually delights in showing mercy, but we have to do what it takes to walk in mercy.

Father God - We thank you for your mercy and forgiveness. Help us have the courage that we need to confess and renounce our sin. Show us the people who you have given us that we can confess to. Reveal any sin that we have been hiding. We want to please you and walk in your forgiveness today.

In the name of Jesus, Amen.

Questions:

1. **Which one of the three things listed is the hardest for you to overcome?** (concealing sin, confessing sin, renouncing sin)

2. **Have you had a person in your life (now or in the past) that you could confess sin to and share accountability with?**

Day 5 - Pardon for You and for Me

"O for the wonderful love He has promised
Promised for you and for me
Though we have sinned, He has mercy and pardon
Pardon for you and for me"

Isaiah 55:6-7 - Seek the Lord while he may be found; call on him while he is near. Let the wicked forsake their ways and the unrighteous their thoughts.

Let them turn to the Lord, and he will have mercy on them, and to our God, for he will freely pardon.

Ephesians 2:4-5 - But because of his great love for us, God, who is rich in mercy, made us alive with Christ even when we were dead in transgressions—it is by grace you have been saved.

"Oh for the wonderful love he has promised, promised for you and for me!" We have such a wonderful love in our God. He loved us even when we were dead in our sins. This is a type of love that you don't have to perform for or be good enough to attain. He loves us simply because that is who He is.

I encourage you today to stop performing for God. Stop thinking that if you do enough good things that He will love you. You either end up feeling hopeless because you didn't do enough or prideful because you think you earned His love and salvation. You don't have to earn His love or attention, it is already yours.

"Though we have sinned He has mercy and pardon, pardon for you and for me." The idea of being pardoned is when you are not held accountable for something that you rightfully deserve. This is what happened through Jesus. He offers pardon for our sin. He took the punishment that should have been handed down to us.

Again, this is something that we cannot earn but that we simply receive.

When we don't see it as a free gift, we don't recognize what grace really is. It is by grace that you have been saved! This is truly the best gift in the world.

Father God - We rest in your love today. Forgive us for performing for you at times instead of simply receiving the love for us that you offer. Your mercy and pardon are true gifts. We don't deserve to be pardoned, but in your goodness you made a way for us to experience true forgiveness and salvation. We praise you for that!

In the name of Jesus, Amen.

Questions:

1. **Is there a time in life where you have pardoned someone?** (Not held them accountable for what they did or said to you)

2. **How does it make you feel to know that Jesus has pardoned you for your sins?**

Week 9: With You Always

SONG FOR THE WEEK - In The Garden

VERSE 1:
I come to the garden alone
While the dew is still on the roses
And the voice I hear falling on my ear
The Son of God discloses
CHORUS:
And He walks with me, and He talks with me
And He tells me I am His own
And the joy we share as we tarry there
None other has ever known
VERSE 2:
He speaks, and the sound of His voice
Is so sweet the birds hush their singing
And the melody that He gave to me
Within my heart is ringing
VERSE 3:
I'd stay in the garden with Him
Though the night around me be falling
But He bids me go; through the voice of woe
His voice to me is calling

Day 1 - He Walks with Me

"And He walks with me, and He talks with me
And He tells me I am His own
And the joy we share as we tarry there
None other has ever known"

Genesis 3:8 - Then the man and his wife heard the sound of the Lord God as he was walking in the garden in the cool of the day, and they hid from the Lord God among the trees of the garden.

Matthew 28:20b - And surely I am with you always, to the very end of the age.

Isn't it encouraging to know that God designed us to live in fellowship with Him? He didn't intend for us to live at a distance from Him. He created us with a void in our heart that only He is capable of filling. When we try to fill that place with other relationships or things, it always falls short.

As Jesus was having His final conversations with His disciples, He wanted to make sure they knew that He would always be with them, even to the very end of the age. I think, at times, we see God more as a religious figure rather than a God who is present in our lives and a God who wants to be in close relationship with us.

God does not love at a distance. He is a personal God who desires to speak to our hearts and lead us in life. We see this idea of God being among His people in the Garden of Eden where God is walking in the garden where Adam and Eve lived. Because they ate the fruit God told them not to eat, they were afraid of God's presence and they hid.

This can happen in our lives at times too. When we sin or live lives that we know don't fully please God it causes us to go into hiding. I encourage you to come out of hiding today! It is never too late to reconnect with God and walk in fellowship with Him.

Father God - We thank you that you walk with us and you talk with us. There is a joy that comes from a relationship with you that nothing else can offer. We ask for your forgiveness for areas of sin. We don't want to hide from you or live at a distance from you. Help us to live in full awareness of your love and your presence in our lives. Show us the areas where we have drifted away from that fellowship.

In the name of Jesus, Amen.

Questions:

1. **Did you have the type of dad or mom that you would hide from when you did something naughty as a child? Describe a time when you remember getting into trouble for something when you were a kid.**

2. **Can you recall a time in life (it could be even now) where you kept yourself at a distance from God because you knew your life or behavior didn't please Him?**

Day 2 - I Come to the Garden Alone

"I come to the garden alone
While the dew is still on the roses
And the voice I hear falling on my ear
The Son of God discloses"

Mark 1:35 - Very early in the morning, while it was still dark, Jesus got up, left the house and went off to a solitary place, where he prayed.

Matthew :6 - But when you pray, go into your room, close the door and pray to your Father, who is unseen. Then your Father, who sees what is done in secret, will reward you.

1 Chronicles 16:11 - Look to the Lord and his strength; seek his face always.

There is something about spending time alone with God. The author of the hymn 'In the Garden' understood the importance of alone time with God writing, "I come to the garden alone, while the dew is still on the roses." This portrays the idea of coming to God so early in the morning that there is still dew on the flowers.

Jesus modeled this lifestyle for us. All throughout scripture we see Him spending time alone with God. He also had a core group of people in His life (His disciples) but He knew He still needed time and space where it was just Him and His Father.

Spending time with God alone must be done intentionally. In Mark 1 it says that Jesus got up very early, while it was still dark, and left the house to find a solitary place. When was the last time that you got up while it was still dark to spend time with God? For most of us, we probably wouldn't be able to recall that moment.

We don't need to be legalistic about getting up at a certain time or doing things a certain way, but there is significance to the idea of putting God first in our day before anything else. As we spend time alone with God first thing in the morning it prepares us for what the day will bring.

Father God - We long for a connection with you. A personal connection that is not only something we experience through other people but a connection that we have directly with you. Forgive us for not making the space to spend alone time with you and direct us on how to do that better moving forward.

In the name of Jesus, Amen.

Questions:

1. **Have there been people in your life that did a good job of spending time alone with God?**

   a. **What did it look like for them?**

2. **How do you spend time alone with God?**

   a. **Is this an area that you could grow in?**

Day 3 - The Sound of His Voice

"He speaks, and the sound of His voice
Is so sweet the birds hush their singing
And the melody that He gave to me
Within my heart is ringing"

Psalm 29:4 - The voice of the Lord is powerful; the voice of the Lord is majestic.

Revelation 3:20 - Here I am! I stand at the door and knock. If anyone hears my voice and opens the door, I will come in and eat with that person, and they with me.

During one of my visits at a patient's home, I noticed a beautiful work of art hanging on the wall. It was a picture of Jesus standing at a door and knocking. My patient's husband, we'll call him Robert, was talking to me about how God speaks to his heart and he said, "It is like this painting of Jesus. It dawned on me the other day that there is no door handle on the door where Jesus is knocking. I thought that was odd until I realized that the handle is only on the inside of the door."

Robert completely understood the intention behind this painting. It is meant to teach us that Jesus stands at the door of our heart and knocks, but He will not force Himself in. It is up to us to open the door. This is how the voice of God works. He pursues us. He stands at the door of our hearts and knocks, but He waits for us to respond to His voice.

Father God - We thank you that you stand at the door of our heart and knock. We thank you for speaking to us directly. We give you access to every area of our hearts. We open up our hearts to you entirely today.

In the name of Jesus, Amen.

Questions:

1. **How do you hear the voice of God in your life?**

2. **At what age did you first open the door to Jesus in your heart? Have you had to reopen that door or has it stayed open?**

Day 4 - He Bids Me Go

"I'd stay in the garden with Him
Though the night around me be falling
But He bids me go; through the voice of woe
His voice to me is calling"

Matthew 28:19-20 - Therefore go and make disciples of all nations, baptizing them in the name of the Father and of the Son and of the Holy Spirit, and teaching them to obey everything I have commanded you.

Psalm 32:8 - I will instruct you and teach you in the way you should go; I will counsel you with my loving eye on you.

The last verse of the song 'In the Garden' says, "I'd stay in the garden with Him...but he bids me go." When I sing these words it reminds me that while my alone time with God is essential in my life, I am not meant to stay alone with God forever. After spending that time alone with Him, He then sends me out to be with others.

Each one of us has a similar mission in life and that is to make disciples of Jesus. This means that we tell people about what Jesus has done in our lives and we teach them how to obey what Jesus has commanded. The people that God has called us to might be family members, staff members or other residents at a facility, neighbors, friends, etc.

No matter where we find ourselves in life we should always be on a mission to make disciples of Jesus. We can be encouraged knowing that God will instruct us in the way that we should go. It can be overwhelming to think about who we are supposed to talk to about Jesus, but we can trust that God will direct us in that. All we need to do is have a heart that says yes!

Father God - We thank you for entrusting us with the best news of all time, The Gospel of Jesus! Show us who you want us to introduce you to and show us how to teach them to follow and obey you. We surrender ourselves to be sent out today!

In the name of Jesus, Amen.

Questions:

1. **How did you come into a relationship with Jesus?**

2. **Did someone spend time teaching you how to obey the commandments of Jesus?**

3. **Are there people God is asking you to share the gospel with in your life now? Who?**

Day 5 - He will Uphold You

Isaiah 41:10 - So do not fear, for I am with you; do not be dismayed, for I am your God. I will strengthen you and help you; I will uphold you with my righteous right hand.

Romans 8:38-39 - For I am convinced that neither death nor life, neither angels nor demons, neither the present nor the future, nor any powers, neither height nor depth, nor anything else in all creation, will be able to separate us from the love of God that is in Christ Jesus our Lord.

When we realize that God is always with us, it should remove fear from having a grip in our lives. We don't have to fear the unknown of what's ahead because we know the one who will be with us.

We also need to remind ourselves that no matter what we go through in this life there is nothing that can separate us from the love of God. Not even death can separate us from the love of Christ.

I have spent many final moments with people and at times there is a level of fear and anxiousness leading up to a person's final breath. If you find yourself in that fear today, I want to encourage you that the love of God will walk you through the entire process. You cannot fully know what lies ahead of you on that journey, but you can be certain that God will be with you, He will help you and strengthen you, He will uphold you, and His love will be with you each step of the way.

Father God - Thank you for your continual strength and support. Thank you that even at the hour of my death you are with me and that your love surrounds me. Help me let go of fear and replace it with total trust in you.

In the name of Jesus, Amen.

Questions:

1. **Did you grow up in a house that had a lot of fear or was it mostly peaceful? Take a moment to explain.**

2. **Are there things that you fear today?**

Week 10: Fix Your Eyes

SONG FOR THE WEEK - Turn Your Eyes Upon Jesus

VERSE 1:
O soul, are you weary and troubled
No light in the darkness you see
There's light for a look at the Savior
And life more abundant and free
CHORUS:
Turn your eyes upon Jesus
Look full in His wonderful face
And the things of earth will grow strangely dim
In the light of His glory and grace
VERSE 2:
Through death into life everlasting
He passed, and we follow Him there
O'er us sin no more hath dominion
For more than conqu'rors we are
VERSE 3:
His Word shall not fail you, He promised
Believe Him and all will be well
Then go to a world that is dying
His perfect salvation to tell

Day 1 - Turn Your Eyes

"Turn your eyes upon Jesus
Look full in His wonderful face
And the things of earth will grow strangely dim
In the light of His glory and grace"

1 Corinthians 13:12-13 - For now we see only a reflection as in a mirror; then we shall see face to face. Now I know in part; then I shall know fully, even as I am fully known. And now these three remain: faith, hope and love. But the greatest of these is love.

Hebrews 12:1b-2 - And let us run with perseverance the race marked out for us, fixing our eyes on Jesus, the pioneer and perfecter of faith. For the joy set before him he endured the cross, scorning its shame, and sat down at the right hand of the throne of God.

Scripture uses the picture of a race to refer to this life. If someone was running a race but they had no idea where the finish line was, or simply just chose not to look at the finish line, they would run aimlessly. They would end up exhausted and likely never reach the finish line.

It is the same when it comes to our faith. We need to keep our eyes fixed on Jesus who is the author and the one who perfects our faith. If we wander through this life looking at whatever grabs our attention, then we will be wandering aimlessly.

It is true that now we only see the things of eternity as a reflection in a mirror and one day we shall see face-to-face. We now know in part, but one day we shall know fully and be fully known. In the meantime, we need to 'run this race' well and we only do that as we keep our minds and our focus on Jesus.

Pursue Jesus with all of your heart. Talk to Him each day. Find ways to read or listen to scripture. Sing hymns and spiritual songs to Him. All of these are ways to keep your eyes fixed on Jesus. When something else wants your attention, be sure to quickly correct your focus back to Jesus and stay the course.

Father God - We know that now we only know partly but we anticipate the day that we will be with you face-to-face. Help us keep our eyes fixed on you so that we can finish this race that you have assigned us to well. We love you, Lord.

In the name of Jesus, Amen.

Questions:

1. **Analogies are so helpful in helping us understand spiritual things (like a race referring to this lifetime). Did you play sports as a child and/or adult?**

2. **What are some of the distractions in life that try to steal your attention?**

   a. **Has that changed over the years?**

Day 2 - More Abundant and Free

"O soul, are you weary and troubled
No light in the darkness you see
There's light for a look at the Savior
And life more abundant and free"

Psalm 119:28 - My soul is weary with sorrow; strengthen me according to your word.

John 10:9-11 - I am the gate; whoever enters through me will be saved. They will come in and go out, and find pasture. The thief comes only to steal and kill and destroy; I have come that they may have life, and have it to the full.

I am the good shepherd. The good shepherd lays down his life for the sheep.

Our souls grow weary and troubled at times. David, the writer of Psalm 119, knew that God was the only source of the strength that he needed. The same is true for us today. When we are weary and troubled, God is able and willing to strengthen us.

John chapter 10 records Jesus speaking about Himself as the "good shepherd." He says that He is the gate to the Kingdom of God and that those who enter through Him will be saved. It is important that we understand that there truly is only one way to eternal life and that is through Jesus. As hard as it is to hear, not all roads lead to eternal life, but thank God that He provided a way through His son, Jesus Christ!

Not only does Jesus provide eternal life to us, He provides a full and abundant life right now! We don't have to walk around with our heads down in defeat. Jesus died and rose again so that we could experience an abundant life and true freedom! If there are areas where you don't feel freedom and peace, I encourage you to walk through the gate of Jesus today into all that God has for you. Tell Him the areas where you need Him to change you and then walk in that freedom!

Father God - Thank you for making a way for us to know you and spend eternity with you through Jesus. We thank you for the strength that you provide to our souls when we feel weary and troubled. We ask that you reveal the areas where we have not fully received the abundant life that you offer.

In the name of Jesus, Amen.

Questions:

1. **In what ways is your heart troubled?**

2. **The weariness described in the scripture above comes from sorrow. Do you feel sorrow over anything right now?**

   a. **How does knowing that Jesus is at the gate of the Kingdom of God help ease that sorrow?**

Day 3 - We Follow Him There

"Through death into life everlasting
He passed, and we follow Him there
O'er us sin no more hath dominion
For more than conqu'rors we are"

Revelation 21:3-4 - And I heard a loud voice from the throne saying, "Look! God's dwelling place is now among the people, and he will dwell with them. They will be his people, and God himself will be with them and be their God. 'He will wipe every tear from their eyes. There will be no more death' or mourning or crying or pain, for the old order of things has passed away."

Romans 8:37 - No, in all these things we are more than conquerors through him who loved us.

I hope that the scriptures we just read fill you with overwhelming hope. We have so much hopeful anticipation for that day when God's dwelling will be among us. He will wipe every tear from our eyes. There will be no more death, mourning, crying or pain. It is hard for us to imagine this sort of existence but that is what awaits those who have received Jesus.

Although we experience difficulties and hardships in this life, we are more than conquerors through Christ. May it fill you with peace as you recognize that nothing can separate you from the love of God that is in Christ Jesus our Lord. Neither death nor life can separate you from the love of God. He walks you through the entire process of transitioning from this life to the next.

My prayer is that as you think about transitioning from this life to the next, that you would not have fear but that you would be convinced that not even death itself can separate you from the love of God. He will not leave you. He will be with you each step of the way and when you finally arrive at your forever home, He will dwell with you and wipe every tear from your eye.

Father God - We are filled with hope and joy as we think about being with you face-to-face. Help us to realize that nothing can separate us from your love. We trust you and believe that you will always be with us.

In the name of Jesus, Amen.

Questions:

1. **How will having God dwell with you directly be different from what you experience now?**

2. **What are some things of eternity that you look forward to the most?**

Day 4 - Believe in the Name of Jesus

"His Word shall not fail you, He promised
Believe Him and all will be well
Then go to a world that is dying
His perfect salvation to tell"

1 John 5:11-13 - And this is the testimony: God has given us eternal life, and this life is in his Son. Whoever has the Son has life; whoever does not have the Son of God does not have life. I write these things to you who believe in the name of the Son of God so that you may know that you have eternal life.

Psalm 103:8 - 8 The Lord is compassionate and gracious, slow to anger, abounding in love.

Before we conclude this devotional I want to encourage you to fully believe in Jesus. It is through Jesus that God has given us eternal life. I have talked to a lot of people who are facing death and they have believed in Jesus for a long time, but moments of doubt enter their minds which causes a little shame because they feel like they should not struggle with doubt at this point in their faith journey. If you resonate with that, I want to encourage you that God can meet you in that place of doubt. Doubt doesn't mean that you don't believe in Jesus, it simply means that you are human. Moments of doubt are very normal, especially as you get closer to eternity.

I am reminded of the story in Mark 9 where there is a boy who was possessed by a demon and the father says to Jesus, "If you can do anything, take pity on us and help us." Jesus replied saying "'If you can'?"... "Everything is possible for one who believes." Mark goes on to say that, "Immediately the boy's father exclaimed, "**I do believe; help me overcome my unbelief!**" (Mark 9:22 -24). That is just it, isn't it! I do believe, but help me overcome my unbelief.

God is faithful to meet us in those places of doubt. Until you see God face-to-face you may have doubt from time to time. Instead of letting shame or fear fill your mind, just talk to God about it. Tell Him that you do believe but that you need Him to help you overcome your unbelief. Remember, our God is compassionate and gracious. You can go to Him without fear and let Him help you in that place of doubt.

Father God - You are so good. We thank you for Jesus and the eternal life that we have through Him. We confess that we have doubt at times. We want to have faith and fully believe in Jesus and the things of eternity so we ask that you would help us overcome our unbelief. We receive the gift of salvation through Jesus.

In the name of Jesus, Amen.

Questions:

1. **Describe a time when you experienced doubt regarding your faith. How did you overcome that doubt?**

2. **Do you see Jesus as the one true way to eternal life?**

Day 5 - The Things of Earth will Grow Strangely Dim

"Turn your eyes upon Jesus
Look full in His wonderful face
And the things of earth will grow strangely dim
In the light of His glory and grace"

Psalm 27:8 - My heart says of you, "Seek his face!" Your face, Lord, I will seek.

2 Corinthians 4:16-18 - Therefore we do not lose heart. Though outwardly we are wasting away, yet inwardly we are being renewed day by day. For our light and momentary troubles are achieving for us an eternal glory that far outweighs them all. So we fix our eyes not on what is seen, but on what is unseen, since what is seen is temporary, but what is unseen is eternal.

There is one line in this song that has always stuck out to me; "And the things of earth will grow strangely dim in the light of His glory and grace." I believe that God wants us to have a deep sense of awareness of the things of eternity while we live here on earth. Our eternal destination is forever. This lifetime is a speck on the timeline of our entire existence. As James says, it is "a mist that appears for a little while then it vanishes" (James 4:14).

We should be more focused on the things of eternity than the things of this life. Although our bodies fail us and outwardly we waste away, inwardly we can be renewed each day as we seek God. There is an eternal glory that is being developed in us through our suffering.

The biggest way that we see things through the lense of eternity is by fixing our eyes on what is unseen because we recognize that what we see is temporary but what is unseen is eternal. When we truly seek God we prepare our own heart for eternity and we also can be used by God to help others wake up to the realities of eternity. There is no existence more important than that!

Father God - We recognize that the things we so often focus on, the things that we can see, are temporary. We want to focus on the things that will last forever. Help us to live lives where we see everything through the lense of eternity and what really matters once we are there with you. There truly is no relationship more important than our relationship with you. Your face Lord, we will seek.

In the name of Jesus, Amen.

Questions:

1. **Have you ever thought about how short this life is in comparison to your forever existence in eternity? How does it make you feel when you reflect on that?**

2. **What are some things that are "seen" and some that are "unseen" that Paul refers to in the passage we read from 2 Corinthians chapter 4?**

3. **What can you do today to prepare your heart for eternity?**

FINAL PRAYER

A prayer to pray as you send someone home:

Father God - We thank you for the life of _____. God you are sovereign and you know when you want to call your child home. We trust you in this journey. God, we ask that you give _____ peace in the deepest level of their soul as they cross from this life into eternity. Help them to feel your constant presence with them and your perfect love that will never leave them. We thank you for Jesus and that through Him we have a way to spend all of eternity with you. Take _____ by the hand and lead them home. Help them know that you are with them each step and that you will not leave them. Holy Spirit give _____'s family peace and comfort that only you can give. Help them know that you see them and that you are with them through this journey. Help them surrender _____ into your hands. Father into your hands we release _____'s spirit. Receive them into your kingdom. In Jesus' name we pray. AMEN.

Made in the USA
Middletown, DE
01 March 2024